Jean

The Bicycles of Ice and Salt

Indigo Dreams Publishing

First Edition: The Bicycles of Ice and Salt
First published in Great Britain in 2021 by:
Indigo Dreams Publishing Ltd
24 Forest Houses
Halwill
Beaworthy
EX21 5UU
www.indigodreams.co.uk

Jean Atkin has asserted her right under the Copyright, Designs
and Patents Act 1988 to be identified as the author of this work.
© 2021 Jean Atkin

ISBN 978-1-912876-64-8

British Library Cataloguing in Publication Data. A CIP record
for this book can be obtained from the British Library.

Designed and typeset in Palatino Linotype by Indigo Dreams.
Cover design by Ronnie Goodyer from author's original
images.
Printed and bound in Great Britain by 4edge Ltd.

Papers used by Indigo Dreams are recyclable products made
from wood grown in sustainable forests following the guidance
of the Forest Stewardship Council.

To Shona, and seven years later, Paul,
very dear companions
of two long winter journeys
by bicycle, long ago.

CONTENTS

The Bicycles of Ice and Salt

The bicycles of ice and salt

Green panniers strapped and hooked to racks
we pedal the east of France, this autumn so bitter
the bicycles grow ice in their chains.

They sing like birds, says a lyrical
bike mechanic in Troyes. He hoses them down
with hot water, and they go quiet.

We ride through white bees of hoarfrost
that blur our eyelashes. Ice narrows us.
We count the centimes

double the bread ration, camp
in a numb cold. In Avignon the mistral
rips up our tent pegs, hurls us south.

We ride till our freewheels tick on a track
to the sea. December, and a beach
washed black by short days.

Glassy waves crash in the dark. We hear them
break. There is no more ice, only a swell
of salt to melt the heart.

Valuables

We bought machines built for men
because the crossbar made them stronger.
We bought small-size men's clothes
and men's cycling shoes, because that
was what there was.

We bought a lightweight tent and split
the inner and pegs, the flysheet and poles
onto each bike. We bought Richard's
Bicycle Book, the one that told you how
to kill a dog with a pump.

We bought nothing that explained how
to travel through the world of men.
We weren't streetwise. We had to learn
how to look competent, avoid their eye,
how and when to lie.

Auxerre motel

The campsite closed, we find a room
in a roadside motel. La patronne

is suspicious, makes us pay up front.
There are cold, tiled corridors,

commercial travellers.
Next morning she sees us

off the premises, scowls
when I drop our jar of jam.

Oxen at Laon

A mile away the famous ox horns double-branch
from each cathedral tower. But cycling in

at horse-speed, we find wood scaffolding
overleans the dirty streets.

The towers reach ambitious, incomplete,
into shifting cloud. We pass by

the bony oxen, who remember
every century. We see the women

are keeping their eyes down.
We ride past carts and carts of stone.

Vive la vélorution

We didn't so much plan, as bolt.
Out of England, out from under
everything. We didn't even know
all the things we didn't know.

Slowly we tacked our ramshackle days
into something we hadn't known
the shape of, had never
had a pattern for.

As it turned out, we'd set off riding
on the means of production.
We rebuilt ourselves.

Eve in Autun

Young and shivering I stand in front of Eve
who's any age, and beautiful, in stone.
Her naked body's sinuous as trees. This
is about the flesh, and not the bone.

The nave's deep cold threads through
my clothes. I breathe the longings in its walls.
I'm half in love with this woman made
of stone, not lewd, about to fall.

She lies in the Garden, in the leaves, one hand
to her soft cheek as she whispers to Adam.
Her breasts hang round as fruits. I watch her reach back,
without looking, for the apple and her whoredom.

Grass verge near Soissons

Under wheels, leaves flash a fallen sunlight
in the lanes. Cold farms
are hung with hoarfrost

and stiff sheets. We stop for water
by an orchard, pinch two pears
from over the ditch.

Their skins are bronze,
a little rough,
flesh sweet.

Monpazier

We stop for lunch in this arcaded bastide town.
The Fête de la Toussaint has closed the shops.
Only a small boy, who shows us
his bike, and then the medieval measures,
from whose bronze pans
he looks forward, soon, he says,
to the eating of sweet chestnuts.

Jeremiah dances

Jeremiah moves on his toes, beside
heraldic lions stepped up on one another's backs.
The lions are very still

but Jeremiah dances. His head and shoulders sway
in dreamlike opposition to his turning step.
Clinging pleats flow over his long legs.

Even his bare feet are long: bones flexed
yet barely treading earth. He holds in his hands
a scroll he does not read.

We stand at Moissac with a bike pump and a baguette.
He holds us in his tender gaze.
Here's a face that has seen trouble.

I see a seething pot says Jeremiah. *How long
shall the land mourn and the herbs of every field
wither for the wickedness of them?*

Stone streams through his hair and beard. He says,
*The joy of our heart is ceased; and our dance
turned into mourning.*

But he dances on. His grave and tilted face
now blogged and global, his sorrow
speaking to so many.

Penknives

A December midnight, somewhere
on the Rhone. We lay in sleeping bags
in a closed-down campsite
by the village edge,
rigid

listening to footsteps and voices
more than one man
circling the tent.

We took out our penknives, meant
to use them.

Except, at last,
that silence fell
again.

We cursed them all, meant
every word.

Miel de pays

Kind people sent us to the open common by the river
backed onto their vegetable plots. We camped by the footbridge,
close to the white path and the public water pump.

You sat and read our Penguin Wilkie Collins.
I stirred the bubbling pan.
The Chateau de Padern turned redder, wilder, on its cliff.
Night was falling. There was still birdsong.

Over the footbridge strolled a young man. He sang
beneath his breath in words I didn't understand. By our tent
he halted, and put a jar of honey in my hands.

Camping at Prayssac

Elderly farmers invite us to camp
in their orchard. They help us
get water from the pump.
He says, "Fumez pas, hein?"
We reassure him

but it's a private joke.
He shows us his barn, watches us
take in, high and dim,
the slow spin of long yellowed leaves
strung from each huge beam.

Leaf night

The spokes are going round so slowly I can count them.
The wind bangs like pans in my head.
Leaves cartwheel down the lane towards us.
The frost has licked it clean.

Tonight I know each rattling leaf, spun
from the plane trees of every village square.
Like sails they lift, they scrape and flap.
I can't hear your voice above the gale.

Gusts slam my eyelids so I don't see it start.
A thousand leaves rise up like bolts of cloth.
They rustle as they come for us. I call out your name
just once before they close my mouth.

Leaf day

The instant we turn across the gale by Thézan's vineyards
and little hills, our silent tailwind transforms into a shriek.
Wind pours into our ears like water, drowns our thoughts
we fight to hold the bikes to tarmac, miss the ditch –
which now I see is lined with plane trees.

On sight, their leaves howl through the air
to catch us in the road. They dizzy us.
They slam our spokes and dive.

Large as an elephant's ear, a leaf snags in your brakes
and stops you. It's veined and red and leathery.
I reach down and drag it clear.

At Saintes-Maries-de-la-Mer

In the black of the crypt, Sara la Kali
is wrapped in silk and satin.
In bright wind on the saltmarsh,
a white horse's rolling eye.
We ride onto the beach at last light.
Tyres slide in sand. We make
a ritual, and dip
each bicycle's front wheel
into the sea.

Real at last

In autumn the bicycle teaches me
a culture of fire. The towns are woodsmoked.
Our stolen apples taste of the cold night.

Bitten tarmac unrolls behind our tyres
a trail of work-worn villages and blank-eyed stares.
We tear a baguette under the hedge

and knife a Camembert and pitch
the small green tent each fifty miles,
toothpaste and spit into frost-hung air.

My gear-changes grow smooth. I start
to hunt red courage of the road.
We lift October spiders from our hair.

Medieval lips and vast demonic teeth
engulf the columns at Cunault
and death is real and risk is real at last.

bicycle

i.m. Flann O'Brien

I have perhaps exchanged
  some molecules with it on the road
    so its taut steel has sprung
      my wrists

      & in the same gear
      the flexion of its pedals over tarmac
      has come to seem as natural as feet,
      rhyme and beat of passage

   & in a higher gear
  our wheels map contours
 so we share exhilaration
at the downtilt of a pass

El Vilosell

An old man and a boy are mending a moped.
Beside them, a loaded donkey droops.

Bon Dia, I say, and keep both hands on the bars
because the bike is weaving on the rutted track.

They look up, and the man hasn't shaved
and I think they're both too surprised to speak.

For five minutes the hamlet is a maze we wander,
repetitions of pantiles, propped doors and smoke

and then for an hour we climb through terraces of olives.
Lean men beat the trees with sticks, and fruits rain

into nets through the mesh of their shouts. Cliffs are hawks
rising. We kiss on the brink, and feel, as much as see

the thousand soundless feet of air
falling from here to the Rio Monsant.

Bareheaded in Barcelona

I brake hard as the motorbike fishtails
across three lanes of traffic, right in front.
For a second, meet her dark gaze
as she sways behind her man.
Their bike roars and banks

she lays down her cheek on his back
and her black hair smokes
above the chromed exhaust.
The avenida swallows them.

Roundabout

Across lanes, between lorries, I catch
one glimpse of the terrified dog
that someone has tied by its neck,
with wire, to the roadsign
to Begues in the centre
of the roundabout
its mouth wide open
making no sound
in the roar.

The royal tombs

They lie, crowned, with their hands crossed,
the Kings and Queens of Aragon.
Life-size and cold, they stretch on marble slabs above our heads.
The Monastery of Poblet is paving stones and dust.

A garlicky brother shows us the old dormitory.
He waits while we add our steps
to its echoes, leave our breath on its empty stage.
He blesses us; the folds of his sleeve are green with age.

Rodoñya

Which had no road.
Whose dull yellow houses

watched like eyes its mud streets
of the same colour.
There seemed

to be only ghosts,
but when we picnicked
by the locked church, a black-clad

woman shuffled out in her slippers
to wish us *Bon Dia*.

The lady of Elche

Tailgating in drizzle, the road train of artics
traps us to the gutter. We steer the tarmac edge,
weave roadkill and glass. Between the front wheels
and the rear, they suck you in, and if you live
to see the plates, they blow you back.

We are riding to the palm forest of Elche, where
there are dates in baskets, and palm leaves
are charms against lightning.
Struck deaf by traffic we turn in
by the gates of Huerto del Cura.

Inside the walls we buy sanctuary, a ticket
with a perforated edge. Palm leaves
drip soft warm rain. Ponds dimple.
There is the slow sound of foreign flowers.
The small stone eyes of La Dama de Elche calm us.
Her hair is impossibly braided.

Pensión Olympia, Granada

It was cheap, clean and large, just off the Gran Via.
It was first floor, had an iron balcony we could cook on.
It had a *cama de matrimonio*, bare floorboards
and no heating. It had a lovely landlady in a pinny.

We bought La Ina sherry, Valdepeñas wine, a tin
of artichoke hearts, a tin of anchovies. We bought
Campbell's Luxury Lobster soup, pâté, cheeses,
bars of Turrón and spa water from Lanjarón.

Next day we ate it all, in bed. Later our landlady
offered us her phone, and Christmas greetings.
All the time we talked to England, she handed us
her *dulces de almendra* and small, fierce glasses of brandy.

Holy water

Above Ubrique, Benaocaz; a late December afternoon.
Our narrow road a ribbon into green
and staircased up above, the jagged mountains.
At the roadside a spring that tumbled
in a basin. Lettered above the falling water
FUENTE SANTA.

A woman filled her line of plastic bottles.
We asked about the water. She straightened up: it was
not merely fit to drink, but blessed.
In turn we filled our bottles, sat cross-legged
on the sheep-cropped grass, and drank
until the mountains poured us out.

Lost and found at the Palacio da Pena

A golden dome and battlements
rise out of mist. February, and
the stucco sweats with moss.

We are in a cloudy court
of wet-shined chequered
tiles. Tangled small rooms

are crammed with chairs
and dusty letters, pen nibs
and little mirrors.

Later, in the pensão
we will cut each other's hair,
and leave behind our scissors.

Ponte de Lima

These viridian fields where women are working
with sickles and oxen.
We see the women are washing clothes
in wells and fountains.
And on the banks of the green Lima,
the legions were afraid
to cross, believing they'd forget
their names and their homes
when they stepped
into its waters.

The importance of the roads

Importancia de las carreteras, Michelin 990

Autopista, forbidden to bicycles.
Carretera, with two wide lanes,
very hostile to bicycles.

Obstáculos, road closed
at certain times. Once washed away
by flood, once buried by landslide.

Carretera en mal estado, road in a bad
state. Peaceful places, often signed
'Obras', suggesting repair.

Michelin 990, *España/Portugal*,
stained along the fold, inked nightly
with triangles, direction of our road.

Acknowledgements

Thanks are due to editors of the following publications, in which some of these poems first appeared: The North, And Other Poems, The Ofi Press, Ink, Sweat and Tears, ArtemisPoetry, Atrium and Poetry Salzburg.

'Real at Last' was Highly Commended in the Bristol Poetry Prize in 2015.

Also by Jean Atkin:

Fan-peckled, 2021, Fair Acre Press.
Understories, 2019, Whalebone Music.
How Time is in Fields, 2019, IDP.
Luck's Weight, 2014, Biscuit Tin Press.
The Henkeeper's Almanac, 2013, Biscuit Tin Press.
Not Lost Since Last Time, 2013, Oversteps Books.
The Dark Farms, 2011, Roncadora Press.
Lost at Sea, 2010, Roncadora Press.

Indigo Dreams Publishing Ltd
24, Forest Houses
Cookworthy Moor
Halwill
Beaworthy
Devon
EX21 5UU
www.indigodreams.co.uk